LEADERSHIP SECRETS

SECRETS

from the

EXECUTIVE

OFFICE

GEORGE HATHAWAY

MJF BOOKS
NEW YORK

For Vicki

My advisor, my critic,
My soul, my love,
My wife.
I'm amazed by you...

Published by MJF Books
Fine Communications
322 Eighth Avenue
New York, NY 10001

Leadership Secrets from the Executive Office
ISBN-13: 978-1-56731-632-2
ISBN-10: 1-56731-632-8
LC Control Number 2003115758

Printed in the United States of America.

MJF Books and the MJF colophon are trademarks of Fine Creative
Media, Inc.

VB   12   11   10   9   8   7   6   5

TABLE OF CONTENTS

Introduction

It has been reported that J. Edgar Hoover, the director of the FBI, was once alarmed to discover a rather dramatic increase in FBI activity along the Canadian and Mexican borders with the United States. When he investigated, Hoover found the problem.

It turns out that a month or so earlier his secretary had asked him to edit one of his memos she had just typed up. She wanted him to correct any errors before she sent it off to the FBI field offices. When he finished his edits, Hoover observed that the margins of the note were uneven. So, he wrote, "watch the borders" at the bottom of the memo and gave it back to his secretary to correct and distribute. She logically assumed that Hoover's "watch the borders" comment was some special intelligence alert to the border patrol officers that was to be added to the message.

Most managers will never have the impact on world events that J. Edgar Hoover did. However, all managers, throughout their careers, will be surprised to discover that the results of their behavior are not always what they intended.

Being an effective leader is a demanding challenge. If you've been in a management position for a while, you already know that it's not as easy as you might have once thought. You know that your behavior as a manager can sometimes have unforeseen consequences. Simple comments or facial expressions can trigger ghastly disruptions throughout your organization.

As a manager, then, you might be asking yourself . . .

- ⊕ "Am I as effective a leader as I can be?"
- ⊕ "Am I motivating my employees enough?"
- ⊕ "Am I causing problems I'm not even aware of?"
- ⊕ "Do they understand me?"
- ⊕ "Do they trust me?"
- ⊕ "Are they loyal to me?"
- ⊕ "Do they know how much I truly want them to succeed?"

In over twenty years in management, I have come to understand much of what sets leaders apart from ordinary managers. Drawing on my experience as an employee, and later as a manager and an executive, I have compiled over 130 specific, practical actions that managers can implement on a daily basis to become more effective leaders.

These leadership behaviors are not very complex. In most cases they need little or no explanation at all. And yet, they can make all the difference in the world.

To each entry, I've added quotations from those wiser than I to help make the point—some are humorous, some are serious, but all are insightful.

The hints and tips have been organized into the ten most critical attributes of the successful leader's job. Each chapter contains a brief introduction that will establish a context for the behaviors in the section. I urge you to practice these every day.

Remember, in the long run it's much too easy to be a bad manager. To be a good leader takes a whole lot of hard work and a huge amount of behavior change. So, if you're up for it, get started right away. Begin by changing your attitude.

CHAPTER 1

ATTITUDE

A manager's state of mind has a great deal to do with his or her effectiveness as a leader. When managers are scared, grumpy, or angry, their employees feel uptight and worried. When managers are pleasant, personable, and relaxed, their team is less stressed out.

This chapter identifies behaviors you can adopt right away to improve your attitude and to make others around you feel less pressure.

Chill out . . .

In order to be successful, we managers will work very hard at assuring that the job gets done. But sometimes our intensity creates stress in others around us and has just the opposite effect. Stop driving your people so hard. Chill out and try to have a little fun.

"I always wanted to be somebody, but I should have been more specific."

—Lily Tomlin

Don't take yourself too seriously

For most of us, nothing we are doing today will make any bit of difference in the world a hundred years from now. So, why take things so seriously? Relax. Laugh a little. And, more important, learn to laugh at yourself.

⊚

*"Let me tell you something that
we Israelis have against Moses.
He took us 40 years through the desert
in order to bring us to the one spot
in the Middle East that has no oil!"*

—Golda Meir

Keep your spirits up

There is nothing more frightening to people than seeing their leader in a depressed state of mind. No matter how difficult the situation, always maintain a positive attitude and convey your certitude that everything is going to work out just fine.

"Ability is what you're capable of doing.
Motivation determines what you do.
Attitude determines how well you do it."

—Lou Holtz

Learn to fail

Tom Peters has taught us much. He once said "Learn to fail . . . but fail quickly. . . ." In particular, he tells us to test our ideas before we invest in them. If we're wrong, we should learn from our mistakes quickly before we've gone too far.

"Results!
Why, man, I have gotten a lot of results.
I know several thousand things
that won't work."

—Thomas A. Edison

Leave your ego at home

Most managers have achieved their position through hard work, high performance, and recognized success. Now it's time for you to help your employees to work, perform, and succeed. Remember that *your* success is now based on *their* accomplishments.

*"The bigger a man's head gets,
the easier it is to fill his shoes."*

—Henry A. Courtney

Make the coffee

Ever go to the break room and find an empty coffee pot? Someone took the last cup and didn't take time to make a fresh pot. Learn to make coffee. Do it whenever you find the pot empty. Others will notice and may even adopt the habit themselves.

*"You cannot be a leader,
and ask other people to follow you,
unless you know how to follow, too."*

—Sam Rayburn

No screaming

No matter how bad things get, no situation warrants an angry response from a leader. Raising your voice or, worse yet, screaming at someone demonstrates a total lack of self-control. Your team will quickly lose faith in you as their leader. Curb your emotions or you may lose those manager stripes.

⊚

"When faith is lost,
when honor dies,
the man is dead."

—John Greenleaf Whittier

Repeat after me: "I can fix anything"

As a manager, you have a long track record of success behind you. You must continue to develop and demonstrate the confidence that you can fix anything that goes wrong. If you can't fix a problem, do your best to find a resolution, then find the serenity to accept the fact that we live in an imperfect world. Don't get bogged down.

"The man who has confidence in himself gains the confidence of others."

—Hasidic saying

Smile, Boss . . .

Look around you. Who are the people in whom you have the most confidence? It is usually those who are relaxed and confident enough to smile regularly. When the boss smiles, everyone feels better. Give everyone a break and smile, boss.

*"Few things in the world
are more powerful than a positive push.
A smile. A word of optimism and hope.
A 'you can do it' when things are tough."*

—Richard M. DeVos

Take risks

It is reported that Lee Iacocca made decisions with only 60 percent of the information he needed. Talk about your risk takers! He knew that he was going to make mistakes, but he understood that you miss 100 percent of the shots you don't take.

"Chance is always powerful.
Let your hook be always cast;
in the pool where you least expect it,
there will be a fish."

—Ovid

Tell good stories

The world is often too serious a place for us humans. You've been through a lot to get to where you are today, so share some of your more humorous adventures with your staff. Your wit and self-confidence will demonstrate just how human you really are.

*"A sense of humor
is part of the art of leadership,
of getting along with people,
of getting things done."*

—Dwight D. Eisenhower

Chapter 2

Sensitivity

Every good leader understands the fact that his or her employees are, first of all, human. They have feelings. They want to be treated with respect. They have opinions that must be heard. They know that they are not perfect, but they are good people who deserve to be treated as such.

This chapter identifies specific behaviors you can adopt to become more sensitive to the feelings of your employees.

Don't play favorites

People are very sensitive to how a manager differentiates his or her employees from one another. They are always looking for signs of favoritism. Do your very best not to act in a way that signals your preference for one employee over another. Small steps like remembering to alphabetize all distribution lists will keep everyone guessing.

⚛

"Even the hint of prejudice of any type has no place in a well-run organization."

—Fred A. Manske, Jr.

Return phone calls

Isn't it annoying when someone fails to return your phone call? Pay others the respect they deserve—call people back promptly. It is a courtesy that will be greatly appreciated.

*"If a man be gracious
and courteous to strangers,
it shows he is a citizen of the world."*

—Francis Bacon

Attend weddings and funerals

If one of your staff is kind enough to invite you to his or her wedding, try to find the time to attend. If you can't, be sure to send a card and a small wedding gift. When a close relative of one of your employees passes away, make time to attend the funeral and pay your respects to the family. If you cannot be there in person, send a sympathy card and flowers.

🌀

"Always go to other people's funerals, otherwise they won't come to yours."

—Yogi Berra

Close your door

When you have confidential meetings or phone conversations, shut the door so that others will not hear you. This is especially important when you need to discipline a member of your staff.

*"I don't want three million people
digesting my private life
over their cornflakes."*

—Francesca Annis

Don't look at your watch

While meeting with members of your staff, looking at your watch is rude. They might get the idea that your time together is over, or worse, that you're not interested in what they have to say. Show how much you respect them and keep your attention focused on them.

@

*"Either this man is dead
or my watch has stopped."*

—Groucho Marx

Don't swear

No matter how stressful or emotional a situation may be, avoid using profanity in the workplace. You never know whom you might offend.

🌀

*"There ought to be a room
in every house
to swear in."*

—Mark Twain

No sudden moves

When you're first assigned as the manager of a department, your team will be watching your early moves. They will be skeptical of your motives because they are worried about their future. Don't make any sudden moves. Take time to survey the landscape. Identify what's working as well as what needs to be fixed. Seek suggestions about actions that may be required and then ask the team to help you make improvements.

❧

"The art of progress is
to preserve order amid change."

—Alfred North Whitehead

Don't answer that phone

When someone is spending time with you in your office and your phone rings, don't interrupt the discussion to answer the call. If the caller has something more important for you to attend to, your assistant will surely let you know, or you can check your voice mail after the meeting. Demonstrate respect for your visitor and let the call go.

*"The average American worker
has fifty interruptions a day,
of which seventy percent
have nothing to do with work."*

—W. Edwards Deming

Express birthday greetings

A really nice touch for a leader is to remember the birthday of everyone in the department. You don't need a cake; a personal comment to the employee is sufficient. Use computer-calendaring tools to help remind you.

🌀

*"A diplomat is a man who
always remembers a woman's birthday
but never remembers her age."*

—Robert Frost

Get out from behind that desk

No one likes to meet with his or her leader when that leader is ensconced behind a big desk. There are only a few times (if ever) when you must be seated at your desk when meeting or speaking with someone, especially a member of your team. Come out from behind that desk. Use a couple of guest chairs where you and your visitor can sit side by side and talk more casually; it will remind your team that you're one of them.

*"The desk is a dangerous place
from which to watch the world."*

—John le Carré

No dirty jokes

Whether you are male or female, sexual harass-ment is a very serious matter for managers and employees. Ensure that you are never even per-ceived as sexually harassing someone. Don't even joke about it.

"Jests that give pain are no jests."

—Miguel de Cervantes

No public appraisals

Sometimes a situation can develop in a meeting or in a hallway that managers don't like. If your employee is the cause of the problem, don't tell him or her your opinion in public. Ask the person to meet with you in your office. Then let them have it.

⊚

"It is usually best to be generous with praise, but cautious with criticism."

—Author unknown

No smoking!

The health hazards of smoking are widely publicized, and smoking in public has become less and less acceptable. If you're a smoker, demonstrate your sensitivity toward others and don't light up at work.

"Smoking is one of the leading causes of statistics."

—Fletcher Knebel

Tell them how much time you have

Whenever people want to spe nd time with you—whether in a meeting or on the phone—tell them up front how much time you have for them. They'll understand better when it's time for the discussion to end.

〰

"Time flies like an arrow.
Fruit flies like a banana."

—Lisa Grossman

Watch for signals

How does a leader know when someone on the team is unhappy in his or her job? Signals. Some people will suddenly start showing up late or missing days of work altogether. Perhaps their work becomes sloppy. Others may complain about little things. They stop contributing ideas in meetings. Often they are reluctant to accept new assignments or take direction from you. Watch for these signals, then sit the person down for a serious discussion. Find out what is happening and commit to fixing the problem. If he or she won't go along with you, it may be time to help the individual move on.

"Anger is a signal,
and one worth listening to."

—Harriet Lerner

Respect everyone

Above everything else that you do as a manager, you must always demonstrate respect for members of your team and for everyone with whom you come in contact. This is challenging sometimes, especially when things go wrong, but it is a critical ingredient of being an effective leader.

©

"Civilization is a method of living, an attitude of equal respect for all men."

—Jane Addams

CHAPTER 3

STYLE

The most successful leaders inspire their employees by setting an example for them. Most people will mimic their manager's style and behavior. If a boss is always on time for meetings, then her employees will be too. If a boss keeps his shoes shined, then his team will too. As a manager, you must be willing to set the example for your employees if you want them to perform in a certain way.

This chapter describes specific behaviors that you can adopt to truly inspire your team.

Let's play "follow the leader . . ."

People play "follow the leader" all the time. Your staff is constantly observing your leadership attitude, behavior, and style. Stay alert. Be neat. Clean and polish your shoes. Keep your workspace uncluttered. Stay in control. Give your staff a real leader to follow.

🌀

> *"I am a part of all*
> *that I have met."*
>
> —Alfred Lord Tennyson

Decorate your office

Think about it. You're spending a lot of time in a very small space—your office. Make it more comfortable for yourself and for those who visit you. Decorate it. Put up photographs or prints. Place plants on the shelf or in the window. Have a few knickknacks around.

*"In matters of style,
swim with the current;
in matters of principle,
stand like a rock."*

—Thomas Jefferson

 **CHAPTER 3**

Stay in shape

You may not be aware of it, but everyone can see the weight you're putting on. Do what you can to stay fit and trim. Exercise and keep that figure. Make people proud to call you their manager.

⊚

"The body never lies."

—Martha Graham

Answer your own phone

When you're alone in your office and you have the time to do so, answer your own phone. No one is so important that he or she can't do the small stuff now and then. It will save you and your secretary time—and it will impress the heck out of the caller.

*"Modesty may make a fool
seem a man of sense."*

—Jonathan Swift

Do it yourself

Every now and then, do something that your staff never expects you to do. Type your own memo. Send a fax. Make your own copies. It will be a nice break for you, and it will impress your employees. Maybe they'll be inspired to do it themselves next time.

❧

"It is not enough that we do our best; sometimes we have to do what's required."

—Winston Churchill

Fill the candy dish

A very special touch for a manager is to keep a candy dish in an area where visitors will see it. Keep it full of goodies. Everyone likes a little something extra in his or her day—just be careful that your employees don't get addicted!

*"The true measure of a man is
how he treats someone
who can do him absolutely no good."*

—Samuel Johnson

Send holiday greetings

It's always nice to demonstrate a little humanity every now and then—especially at that special time of the year. Send holiday greetings to your employees and their families. And, take a hint, sign the cards yourself . . .

"Sentiment is the poetry of the imagination."

—Alphonse de Lamartine

Get out of your office

Don't expect your employees to always meet with you in your office. Make the effort to stop by their stations every now and then. It's sometimes called "managing by walking about." You'll be amazed at how much more relaxed they will be.

"Remember that
when an employee enters your office,
he is in a strange land."

—Erwin H. Schell

Tell them about yourself

Never hesitate to let your employees know more about you as a person. Tell them a bit about your past. Tell them about the mistakes you've made. Let them in on some of the more humorous aspects of your career. They'll respect you more, and your interactions with them will be more sincere.

*"We should take care
not to make the intellect our god;
it has, of course, powerful muscles,
but no personality."*

—Albert Einstein

Get quoted

One mark of an image maker is having something to say that is worth repeating in the press. But, make certain that you have something of value to say *before* you are asked for your opinion or ideas.

"I often quote myself.
It adds spice to my conversation."

—George Bernard Shaw

Host social events

Whenever you want to demonstrate your appreciation to your team, invite them to a social hour at your place. Don't make it too frequent an event—no more than once a year. And remember, it's deductible!

*"If your capacity to acquire
has outstripped your capacity to enjoy,
you are on the way to the scrap-heap."*

—Glen Buck

Schmooze

There is an important interpersonal art form called "schmoozing." It is the act of engaging in unimportant conversation that imparts nothing and results in no perceptible progress—except the pure demonstration of your own humanity.

❧

*"Do not protect yourself by a fence,
but rather by your friends."*

—Czech proverb

Take them on an excursion or just do pizza

Find opportunities to break away from the frantic pace of the workday. Reduce stress and take your team to a ball game, a concert, a horse race, a movie, a boat ride, or whatever works best. You don't have to leave the office to take a break. Invite the team to join you in relaxing over pizza and soft drinks. It gets everyone away from the normal stresses of the day and gives everyone a chance to communicate with one another.

◎

"There is more to life than increasing its speed."

—Mahatma Gandhi

CHAPTER 4

SALESMANSHIP

A manager's job is to get the work done through others. As such, managers are constantly influencing other people's thinking. This sometimes means that they must convince people to do things they may not want to do. The skill needed to do this well is called salesmanship. Remember the definition of selling: getting others to believe in something as much as you do.

This section lists several behaviors that you will need to acquire to become a successful salesperson.

Be humble

When we are first anointed with the position of manager, we often make the mistake of thinking that we were picked to lead because we were smarter than everyone else. To be really successful as leaders, however, we must maintain a degree of humility and accept that others often have better solutions than we do.

🌀

*"If I only had a little humility,
I'd be perfect."*

—Ted Turner

Be nice

If you're hoping that your employees will accept your ideas, remember they will have a very difficult time agreeing with you if you've treated them badly. Give your ideas their fair shake and be nice to your staff. Your mother was right all along . . .

*"People buy from
the people they like."*

—IBM sales philosophy

CHAPTER 4

Never argue with your boss

Yes, you can disagree with your manager. You might debate with him or her. You might even get angry with the boss. But never get into a heated argument; it's one you cannot win. So, offer polite comments, then let it go.

❧

"Never argue with a fool.
Someone watching may not be able
to tell the difference."

—Anonymous

Never say "No"

The worst word in the English language is the word "No." Managers use it far too often. Either allow people to do what they believe is best, or find another way of saying "No."

⊚

"Few things help an individual more than to place responsibility upon him, and to let him know you trust him."

—Booker T. Washington

Open your door

Unless you require privacy, let people know that they are welcome to stop by and talk with you. An open door signals "I'm open for business—Come on in."

"The man who lives for himself is a failure;
the man who lives for others
has achieved true success."

—Norman Vincent Peale

Point your desk toward the door

There is a very simple way to let people know that they are welcome in your office. Point your desk toward the door so that people see your face when they enter. Don't turn your back to them—it sends a negative signal.

*"Small cheer and great welcome
makes a merry feast."*

—William Shakespeare

Sell—all the time

When you need to convince someone to adopt your point of view (selling, negotiating, leading, etc.), remember that selling others doesn't begin until they don't agree with you. Take charge, and put your powers of influence to the test.

*"Salesmanship begins
when the customer says 'No.'"*

—IBM sales philosophy

Sell your socks off

Managers do a lot of selling. They must constantly endeavor to influence other people's thinking. It's very hard work, but throw yourself into the job. You must infect others with your enthusiasm and get them to believe in something as much as you do.

*"Enthusiasm is
the very propeller of progress."*

—B. C. Forbes

Take someone to lunch

Every now and then, offer to take a member of your team to lunch. It does not have to be for any particular reason, but some one-on-one time will make you a bit more personable. You'll learn more about your team, and they'll appreciate you more as their leader.

❧

"We are all here on earth to help others; what on earth the others are here for I don't know."

—W. H. Auden

The customer *is* always right

Yes, this is a very old (and tired) business maxim. But it's amazing how few people adhere to it. Remember, most everyone with whom you come in contact is your "customer." So treat everyone as if they are right and your success will be assured.

〰

*"Be everywhere, do everything,
and never fail to astonish the customer."*

—Macy's motto

CHAPTER 5

MOTIVATION

One of the most important roles of an effective leader is to motivate his or her people. Really good leaders work hard at assuring that their employees are self-confident, feel good about their contributions, and are well rewarded for positive results.

Listed in this chapter are behaviors that will help you to become an effective motivator.

Be the coach

Being an effective leader requires that you wear many hats. One of the most important jobs you have is to be your team's coach. Teach them what they need to know. Show them by example. Establish your game plan. Organize your players. Encourage their performance. And, most important, reward them for their success.

"The speed of the boss is the speed of the team."

—Lee Iacocca

Catch 'em bein' good

A good leader generates a healthy, productive spirit in his or her department by seeking opportunities to express appreciation for a job well done. It's easier than you think and very effective.

"Appreciation is a wonderful thing:
It makes what is excellent in others
belong to us as well."

—Voltaire

Don't manage people

Too often, managers treat people as inanimate objects. The best leaders inspire people, but manage tasks. Inform people of the objectives they need to achieve, and then give them space to do their job. You'll be amazed at the results.

"People can't be managed; people must be led."

—H. Ross Perot

Don't praise lightly

Sometimes managers think that praising employees for everything they do makes people happy with their boss. But it's a little like crying wolf. If you praise your people all the time, they won't know when you really mean it. Express appreciation only when it's really deserved.

*"He who praises everybody,
praises nobody."*

—Samuel Johnson

Don't wait for
Administrative Professional's Day

Really good leaders appreciate the value of their secretaries and/or assistants—to themselves and to their organization. Show them how important they are and thank them for the good work they do. You don't need a special day to do it.

*"To keep a lamp burning
we have to keep putting oil in it."*

—Mother Teresa

Help employees to improve

When an employee is not performing on the job, real leaders step up and work with the employee to correct his or her behavior. There are several benefits to doing this, not the least of which are improved work results and happier employees.

*"He that will not give some portion
of his ease, his blood, his wealth,
for others' good, is a poor, frozen churl."*

—Joanna Baillie

Make new employees feel welcome

Have you ever shown up for your first day on a job and found that your new boss has not spent any time preparing for your arrival? Don't let your new employees down. Set up their workspaces for them. Have a "to do" list ready for them. And be sure to introduce them to the team.

❧

"A great leader
never sets himself above his followers
except in caring responsibilities."

—Jules Ormont

Manage by exception

A great way to let your team know that you have confidence in them is to assume all is well. If they have a problem, they'll let you know. Some employees have difficulty escalating problems to their boss; this is where a one-on-one meeting will be helpful.

※

"I always prefer to believe
the best of everybody—
it saves so much trouble."

—Rudyard Kipling

CHAPTER 5

Measure performance regularly

Imagine what it would be like if every now and then someone told you honestly and fairly what they thought of the job you were doing and what you could do to improve—especially if it was early enough to change your habits. Help your employees succeed; review their performance with them every four to six months.

*"Do not wait for the last judgment.
It takes place every day."*

—Albert Camus

Plan their future

A real frustration for employees is not knowing "where all this is leading." When they don't have a career plan for their future, they won't be as productive today. Spend time with each employee to help them plan their future with the company. They'll feel much better about their work today, and a leader could be in the making.

"In preparing for battle
I have always found that plans are useless,
but planning is indispensable."

—Dwight D. Eisenhower

Praise employees in public

When employees accomplish something worth praising, be certain to let them know how pleased you are. Better yet, do it in public. They will feel proud of their work, and your team will be even more motivated than ever.

꩜

*"Get someone else to blow your horn
and the sound will carry twice as far."*

—Will Rogers

Put your people first

Poor managers often make demands of their employees that focus too much on what's best for the business. Sometimes these demands (such as cancelled vacations, late hours, weekend duty, etc.) are bad for the employee, especially when they occur too often. Maintain respect for your employees and their personal lives—put your people first.

⑨

*"The reason most major goals are not achieved
is that we spend our time
doing second things first."*

—Robert J. Mckain

Reward a job well done

The best leaders implement an active and visible reward program within their departments. Public "pats on the back" are always effective, but cash and mementos are powerful motivators. Regardless of how you do it, find time to recognize a job well done.

〇

*"The highest reward for a person's toil
is not what they get for it,
but what they become by it."*

—John Ruskin

Schedule "casual days"

This is more the rule than the exception today. At any rate, be sure to declare "casual days" on a regular basis. It will give everyone a chance to relax more on the job and have a little fun.

🌀

*"Trouble is only opportunity
in work clothes."*

—Henry J. Kaiser

Set clear, measurable goals

Too often, job performance objectives are vague and general. Help your employees succeed by setting goals that have clear, identifiable measures by which they can be evaluated.

*"Management by objective works—
if you know the objectives.
Ninety percent of the time you don't."*

—Peter Drucker

Tell them what you expect

Can you imagine what it would be like if we always had to guess what our manager expected us to accomplish? Don't let your team down. Be tough and to the point. Tell each of them what you expect of them and how you want them to perform on the job.

🌀

"Blessed is he who expects nothing,
for he will never be disappointed."

—Benjamin Franklin

CHAPTER 6

COMMUNICATION

Many people believe that effective communication is the key to success in our world today. The best leaders constantly seek ways to get their message out, to articulate their vision, and to listen to others' ideas.

This chapter lists those behaviors that will help you become a more effective communicator.

Maintain a clear vision

Few people in this world are true visionaries. However, you can provide strong, clear direction to your employees when you articulate for them where you believe they and their business are headed. Let everyone know how the world will look after you get there together.

"Is there anything worse than being blind? Yes, a man with sight and no vision."

—Helen Keller

Be clear and precise

Most managers will be easily frustrated when their employees behave differently than expected. Maybe they didn't understand what you asked of them. It is your job to be clear and precise in your communication with them. It's not their job to decipher what you say.

❋

*"Understanding is
a two-way street."*

—Eleanor Roosevelt

Check your messages often

Being a busy manager doesn't excuse you from certain responsibilities. When people try to reach you by phone or email, respond to their messages. Do it at least twice a day. You'll earn more respect, and you might even learn something critical to your success.

"You will never find time for anything. If you want time, you must make it."

—Charles Buxton

Hold one-on-one meetings

Private, weekly meetings with each member of your team will go a long way toward improving communication. It will also strengthen your working relationship with your employees.

*"We have two ears and one tongue
so that we would listen more
and talk less."*

—Diogenes

Distribute good books

Ever read a book that generates new ideas or helps crystallize your thoughts? When you do, think about getting a copy of that book for each of your employees. It will help you to reinforce your vision, strategy, or business objectives. Whether they read it or not is up to them.

"A classic is something that everybody wants to have read and nobody wants to read."

—Mark Twain

Keep good notes

It is amazing that more people (especially managers) don't keep good notes in discussions or meetings with others. Few people have such an excellent memory that they can remember everything without writing it down. Remember to file your notes for future reference.

*"Writers seldom write the things they think.
They simply write the things they think
other folks think they think."*

—Elbert Hubbard

Keep your team informed

Your employees need to hear from you on a regular basis. Schedule all-hands meetings once a quarter and direct-report meetings once a week. Set up a standard agenda and be sure that you ask staffers to report on special topics. Throw in a little humor to help package your messages.

*"News is that which comes from
the North, East, West and South,
and if it comes from only
one point on the compass,
then it is a class publication
and not news."*

—Benjamin Disraeli

Learn from your team

You'd be amazed at how smart your employees really are. No good leader knows everything. Successful leaders listen to those who do the job every day. Ask for their input. Welcome the bad news as well as the good. Ask them what they think you should do or what decisions you should make.

"Wise men don't need advice.
Fools won't take it."

—Benjamin Franklin

Ask lots of questions

A good leader is never satisfied with partial information. Inject yourself into any discussion, meeting, or debate. Find out as much as you can. When you attend professional conferences, make a real pest of yourself—ask tons of questions. This kind of active learning will not only reinforce the information to your own benefit, but it will encourage your team to do the same.

"No man really becomes a fool until he stops asking questions."

—Charles Steinmetz

Make listening noises

When you're talking with your employees, it's always good form to let them know that you're listening. Express your understanding and attentiveness with an "uh huh" every now and then. Or, ask them to clarify a point they're making. They need you to listen to their words and ideas.

"A good listener is not only popular everywhere, but after a while he gets to know something."

—Wilson Mizner

Don't beat around the bush

As a manager you will sometimes be reluctant to get right to the point. Maybe you're trying to be delicate in a difficult situation. Maybe you're worried about how the message will be received. People need leaders who tell it like it is—just "give it to me straight, Doc." Don't beat around the bush. Give it to them straight. They'll respect you more for it.

"Courage is doing what you're afraid to do. There can be no courage unless you're scared."

—Eddie Rickenbacker

Package messages

Most large meetings are dull as dirt. When you're responsible for hosting a large meeting for people in your organization, put fun into the agenda. It can be, and should be, both entertaining and informative.

*"If I had no sense of humor,
I would long ago have committed suicide."*

—Mahatma Gandhi

Read everything

Good leaders stay on top of news and information. Take the time to stay abreast of the reading material that crosses your desk each day. Read newspapers, magazines, industry reports and forecasts, new technology journals, books, and above all, stuff your team has prepared for your review.

"I took a speed reading course and read War and Peace in twenty minutes. It involves Russia."

—Woody Allen

Share your thoughts

From time to time, as you read or hear something with a special message for your staff, pass it around. You will convey and reinforce your vision. Your staff will learn more about you and enhance their learning—consistent with yours.

"The books that help you the most are those which make you think the most."

—Theodore Parker

CHAPTER 7

SUPPORT

A good leader is always there to lend support. This is one of the more challenging aspects of the job because a manager is ultimately responsible for the team's results—good and bad. Staying positive and supportive during the bad times, as well as the good, differentiates a successful leader from a poor manager.

In this chapter you'll learn about support techniques that will help you stay the course.

Get in the boat

So, your team is out there on the ocean, and their project boat is taking on water. They're sinking. Don't stand on the dock yelling for them to row faster. As their leader, you must get into that boat with them. Find and fix the leaks; then grab an oar and help them make it to shore safely. Your crew will have a deeper and more profound respect for you because you were ready to go down with them.

"In this business
you either sink or swim or you don't."

—David Smith

Defend your team

From time to time, senior managers or others in your organization may be critical of your staff. Demonstrate your support for them by challenging the criticism and defending your team. If the criticism is justified, take it up with your employees in private.

"If anything goes bad, I did it.
If anything goes semi-good, then we did it.
If anything goes real good, then you did it.
That's all it takes to get people
to win football games for you."

—Bear Bryant

Don't do it

Managers often get to be managers because they were good at what they did. When they become supervisors, they have a tendency to stay active in the old job. After all, it's what they know best. Don't do it. Demonstrate by example, then get out of your team's way and let them be successful.

◉

*"I do not like work
even when someone else does it."*

—Mark Twain

Don't interrupt

Think about how often you, as a manager, interrupt your staff while they're working. Studies have found that 40 percent of an employee's time is spent responding to management interruptions. Give your people a chance. Help them get their work done by staying out of the way. If they need you from time to time, be ready to help them succeed.

✺

*"Trust men and they will be true to you;
treat them greatly and
they will show themselves great."*

—Ralph Waldo Emerson

CHAPTER 7

Don't jump to conclusions

There are two sides to every story. This is a simple but often overlooked fact. When a problem occurs, don't jump to conclusions. What may appear to be true may not be true at all. Before making a decision as to how to handle the problem, be sure to get all the information first.

❧

*"A conclusion is the place
where you got tired of thinking."*

—Arthur Bloch

Give them your home phone number

What does it mean to say that you are committed to solving problems for your team? If you really mean it, then be sure that your staff can contact you outside of business hours. Give them your home number, and they will know that you are prepared to help them solve business problems—day or night.

🌀

*"Unless commitment is made,
there are only promises and hopes . . .
but no plans."*

—Peter Drucker

CHAPTER 7

Help them succeed

Employees need to know that you are there for them. When they tell you that they lack something to help them succeed, make sure you take charge to see that they get what they need. Help them be successful—your success starts with theirs.

〽

*"The biggest sin is
sitting on your ass."*

—Florynce R. Kennedy

Keep your team trained

Improving the skills of your team can sometimes be considered "overhead." Don't make the mistake of shortchanging your people on acquiring the knowledge and skills they need to stay (or get) ahead.

❧

"Good leadership consists of showing average people
how to do the work of superior people."

—John D. Rockefeller

Keep up your skills

No matter how good a leader you may think you are, there is always something new to learn. Take the time each year to attend management training seminars with organizations like the American Management Association (http://www.amanet.org /seminars/) or brush up on your computer skills by attending technology training courses. You need to see training and development as a critical investment in your success as a leader. Do it.

⊚

*"Leadership and learning
are indispensable to each other."*

—John F. Kennedy

Maintain an open-door policy

People need to know that their gripes will get a fair hearing from senior management. An open-door policy (skip-level meeting, etc.) is a great way for people to feel that their manager's manager really cares about them and is willing to resolve their problems. Give them a direct line to you, with no intermediaries.

"Outstanding leaders go out of the way to boost the self-esteem of their personnel."

—Sam Walton

Promote your team

Be sure to tell others how well you think your team is doing. A public show of support demonstrates to your team that you stand behind them 100 percent. It will strengthen the team's belief in the organization and encourage them to do better.

❧

"The deepest principle in human nature is the craving to be appreciated."

—William James

Seek advice

Real leaders want to know how things are going with their people. It is better to hear the news—both good and bad—from your employees first hand. Find out what needs to be corrected, and then act quickly to fix it.

"Stupid people always think they are right. Wise people listen to advice."

—Proverbs 12:15

Solve all problems

If an employee cannot count on you to fix problems or answer tough questions, then whom can they count on? One of the key reasons that managers exist at all is to solve problems. Don't let your people down. Help them succeed!

*"Each problem that I solved
became a rule which served afterwards
to solve other problems."*

—René Descartes

Stay home!

Every now and then, help reduce the tension in your group. Stay home for a day. Either take a vacation day or work from home. Sometimes getting out of people's way can add to their enjoyment of the job. It also lets them know you trust them to do their work when left alone.

"Rest: the sweet sauce of labor."

—Plutarch

CHAPTER 8

DRIVE

At the end of the day, leaders are people who get things done. In the military, leaders are the soldiers counted on to take the hill. In business, leaders are the people who demonstrate the drive needed to produce an effective end result. They don't complain about problems along the way; they just deliver the goods.

In this chapter, you'll learn behaviors that provide the drive your organization expects from you as their leader.

Act decisively

Real leaders assert themselves when opportunities to succeed arise. Avoid a common pitfall of some managers—never wait to be told what to do. Be decisive. Take action. Make decisions. Take risks. Your team will be both impressed with your performance and more confident in you as their leader.

"Fortune befriends the bold."

—John Dryden

Manage the risks

Risk-taking is vital to your success as a leader. To grow and progress you must explore new ideas and take chances. But to do so without managing the downside risk is foolish. Keep your eye on any events, information, and business conditions that can cause failure. Then manage them to succeed.

"Be wary of the man who urges an action in which he himself incurs no risk."

—Joaquin Setanti

Cut meeting time in half

You'd be amazed at what can be accomplished in half the time typically allotted to meetings. Turn one-hour meetings into thirty-minute meetings and see what happens.

❧

*"Meetings are indispensable
when you don't want to do anything."*

—John Kenneth Galbraith

Demand the most

Having hired the best people you can, now set a high standard of performance for them. Be sure that they know that you want them to deliver results of which both you and they can be proud. Ask them to help you create success.

⌾

*"If you refuse to accept
anything but the very best,
you will very often get it."*

—W. Somerset Maugham

Demonstrate commitment

One of the key differences between a manager and a leader is the level of commitment to the success of their people. Managers only talk about their commitment—leaders demonstrate it. When you say that you're committed, be ready to take the actions that will prove it to others.

"Think like a man of action and act like a man of thought."

—Henri Bergson

Don't ever be late

One of the most annoying habits that a manager can develop is being late for meetings and appointments. Show everyone with whom you meet that they are important and show up on time.

"The trouble with being punctual is that nobody's there to appreciate it."

—Franklin P. Jones

Get that monkey off your back

Watch out. From time to time, your employees may try to push a responsibility back onto your shoulders—putting the monkey on your back, so to speak. Don't let it happen to you. Put it back on theirs.

"Leadership:
The art of getting someone else
to do something you want done
because he wants to do it."

—Dwight D. Eisenhower

Stop the fight, Ref . . .

As much as you would hope that there is harmony among your team members, personal conflicts will arise. These disputes might start out as quick flare-ups, but they can easily become long-term issues if you don't step in. Here is a chance for you to put on your referee hat and blow your whistle. Take a time-out to mediate the dispute; then let the parties involved know that you expect the bickering to stop. As an added bonus, you'll likely receive some positive leadership points from the rest of the team.

🌀

*"You can't fight in here . . .
this is the War Room!"*

—President Muffley in *Dr. Strangelove*

Go to the sound of the guns

This is an old military expression. It means that if you intend to succeed, then you must take action. Don't wait for problems to come to you. Anticipate, plan your moves, then "go to the sound of the guns."

⟲

"There is always more spirit in attack than in defense."

—Titus Livius

Keep to the schedule

When you are responsible for a meeting, be sure that it starts and ends on schedule. If people are causing the event to drag on, don't hesitate to help them move things along.

🌀

"Restlessness and discontent
are the necessities of progress."

—Thomas A. Edison

Make things happen

As a manager, you have a good deal of control over events and behaviors in your department. It is ultimately up to you to see that those things that need doing get done. Don't hesitate to exercise your power and get your hands dirty.

"Leadership is practiced not so much in words as in attitude and in actions."

—Harold S. Geneen

Go get the boss

No matter how good you are, you cannot do it all. There will be times when you must get your boss involved in solving problems. Most bosses will be glad to help, and you'll get the benefit of their experience. And your boss will be in the boat with you.

"I feel coming on a strange disease—humility."

—Frank Lloyd Wright

Manage your manager

To control the tendency of other managers to delegate just about every task in the world to you, let your boss know what you can and cannot do. Let your own manager know what your priorities are and tell him or her your capacity to do more— or less.

*"The world is filled with willing people;
some willing to work,
the rest willing to let them."*

—Robert Frost

CHAPTER 9

INTEGRITY

No matter how much managers may know about their business, they must first be honest, trustworthy, reliable, and sincere in their interactions with people. If your integrity is not secure, you will not be successful in getting anyone to do a good job.

This chapter offers a set of practical behaviors you can adopt to ensure that you are acting with integrity.

Don't be transparent

Never pass the buck when bad news has to be communicated to your staff. Don't tell your people that your manager would not support your efforts to take action on their behalf. If you don't like a decision that your manager has made, fight it out with him or her—and go to bat for your folks.

✦

"The buck stops here."

—Harry S. Truman

Keep your word

It often seems easier to promise something (pay raise, promotion, etc.) than it is to affect actions that make certain it happens. Be careful never to make a promise you cannot deliver. Your people will come to see you as ineffective and untrustworthy.

❧

*"What you do speaks so loud that
I cannot hear what you say."*

—Ralph Waldo Emerson

Don't counteroffer

There will be times when one of your workers tells you that he or she has been offered an opportunity to work for another employer. Do not make the mistake of trying to keep that employee with you. Wish him or her good luck and begin termination proceedings.

"In this world it is not what we take up, but what we give up, that makes us rich."

—Henry Ward Beecher

Help them move on

When an employee just can't improve his performance on the job, it may be time to move him out. Think of it as "giving him a chance to succeed elsewhere." Good people are sometimes mismatched in their job responsibilities. Let him find employment where his skills are better matched with the business's needs.

⊚

*"Treat people as if they were
what they ought to be,
and you help them become
what they are capable of being."*

—Goethe

Stay the course

Employees are confused when their boss keeps changing his or her mind. Do your best to stick with a decision. Obviously, if you have to change your thinking because of new information, then do so. But try to keep it to a minimum.

*"Ever notice that
'what the hell'
is always the right decision?"*

—Marilyn Monroe

Never criticize a buddy

Complaining about one of your coworkers is disrespectful at best. At its worst, it's very dangerous and could undermine your position. Your staff will undoubtedly speak with others about what they've heard, and that will come back to haunt you.

🌀

"Remember that nobody will ever get ahead of you as long as he is kicking you in the seat of the pants."

—Walter Winchell

Tell the truth

Managers often find themselves in difficult situations where misrepresenting the facts seems the easiest thing to do. Remember, getting caught in a lie—even a little one—will destroy your credibility.

🌀

"A lie can travel halfway around the world while the truth is putting on its shoes."

—Mark Twain

Never criticize your boss

It is often difficult to hide one's emotions, especially when your boss is not behaving as you'd like. Be careful not to convey your negative feelings to your employees. They could develop a healthy disrespect for you *and* your boss. Or worse, they might start conveying their negative feelings to others.

"Any fool can criticize,
condemn, and complain,
and most fools do."

—Benjamin Franklin

No reprisals

There will be times when you are not happy that an employee of yours has complained to your boss about a decision you've made or a behavior you've displayed. Never take it out on the employee! It is not payback time! Forget about it; fix the problem you created and get on with your work.

⊚

"There is no revenge so complete as forgiveness."

—Josh Billings

Admit your mistakes

No one is perfect. We all make mistakes from time to time. Demonstrate your humanity and acknowledge your mistakes openly. Most of all, apologize for the problem you caused and tell your team that you'll do better next time. You'll be surprised at how much trust and respect you'll earn from them.

*"When I woke up this morning
my girlfriend asked me,
'Did you sleep good?'
I said 'No, I made a few mistakes.'"*

—Steven Wright

CHAPTER 10

RESPONSIBILITY

When it's all said and done, a good leader has fundamental responsibilities that must be maintained. You have to manage the business while you lead the people who make things happen. It's a demanding challenge to juggle so many responsibilities at one time, but it is one that must be met head on.

In this chapter you'll learn about asking the tough questions, maintaining a "to do" list, and picking up trash.

Ask the tough questions

Attending meetings and not asking good, tough questions is a waste of your time, and you fail to learn all you need to know. Be a leader—demand good answers. Your staff will grow accustomed to preparing answers to the difficult questions, and this will only help make everyone more productive.

〽

"Judge a man by his questions
rather than his answers."

—Voltaire

Demand quality results

Ford's quality vision works for any business. One of the hardest tasks for a leader is to keep the team focused on results. It takes a lot of time. It requires constant review and assessment. Often a good manager must be tough and demand quality results in order to lead successfully.

"Quality is job one."

—Ford Motor Company motto

No excuses

Ultimately, as a leader, you are responsible for getting the job done. You cannot blame employees, senior managers, customers, competitors, the economy, the weather, or anything else. If your group fails to achieve its objectives, don't make excuses; be a leader and accept full responsibility for the poor results. But, be sure to learn from the mistakes and lead your team to success next time.

"It is wise to direct your anger towards problems
—not people;
to focus your energies on answers
—not excuses."

—William Arthur Ward

Be a professional

Unfortunately, our world has become too forgiving of its leaders. There is a tendency to turn a blind eye to bad behavior as long as success is achieved. You need to do your part to set a professional tone for everyone around you. Don't engage in office romances. Don't pilfer the supply cabinet. Don't spend money that's not yours. Don't do anything that in any way can be construed as irresponsible behavior. Be a professional.

"The quality of a leader is reflected in the standards they set for themselves."

—Ray Kroc

Hold the line

The headlines are filled with stories about leaders who have lost their moral compass. Always remember, it's a leader's responsibility to draw the line between right and wrong. If you move that line to solve a problem, no matter how small, you'll never be able to put it back where it belongs. It's a slippery slope. Maintain your leadership role and hold the line on responsible behavior.

"You cannot escape the responsibility of tomorrow
by evading it today."

—Abraham Lincoln

Manage today's "to dos"

Staying organized is a tough challenge when you're a busy leader. One effective technique is to keep a short list of things that must be accomplished each day. Set up a priority ranking and try to delegate as much as you can.

✆

"The actions of men are the best interpreters of their thoughts."

—John Locke

Get organized!

Getting yourself organized and under control represents about half the effort in becoming a successful leader. Clear your desk. Manage file folders. Reduce the pile of paper in front of you. Follow the TRAFfic rule for handling papers: Throw it out, Refer it to someone else, Act on it, or File it. When you're under control, everyone feels safer.

"One of the advantages of being disorderly is that one is constantly making exciting discoveries."

—A. A. Milne

Publish schedules and agendas

People need time to plan ahead. Let everyone know where you are at all times. This is crucial for your administrative assistant but can be just as valuable for everyone on your team. It's also important to let people know at least twenty-four hours ahead of time what subjects you intend to cover during upcoming meetings. It will give everyone time to formulate thoughts, ideas, and questions to discuss.

"Next week there can't be any crises. My schedule is already full."

—Henry Kissinger

Minimize the number of meetings

This goes along with reducing management interruptions. Find a way to reduce the number of meetings people need to attend. They will have more time to get their work done, and so will you.

*"Half our life is spent
trying to find something to do with the time
we have rushed through life trying to save."*

—Will Rogers

Make interviews worthwhile

The art of the interview question has been lost somewhere. Learn to ask better questions when hiring new staff. You'll discover more about candidates' qualifications, and they'll be more impressed with you as a leader.

"It is better to know some of the questions than all of the answers."

—James Thurber

Hire the best

If you really want to be a successful leader, hire only the best people. This takes time and is a lot of work, but it pays off in the long run. Don't ever compromise on the quality of your staff—you're the one who will pay the price.

⊚

*"The best executive is
the one who has sense enough
to pick good men
to do what he wants done
and self-restraint enough
to keep from meddling with them
while they do it."*

—Theodore Roosevelt

Don't drink

Remember that managers are in positions of authority and must be ready to make critical decisions at a moment's notice. People will question the focus of such decisions if the manager has had a drink or two during the day. Avoid the potential for such problems and wait until you're off-duty.

*"Once during Prohibition
I was forced to live for days
on nothing but food and water."*

—W. C. Fields

Reserve private time for yourself

Busy managers will never find the time to get non-people things done. Set aside "RESERVED" time on your calendar that will assure you get the time you need. If it's not on your schedule you'll never get to it.

"One hour of thoughtful solitude
may nerve the heart for days of conflict—
girding up its armor to meet the most insidious
foe."

—Percival

Make a "clean sweep"

Every now and then it's important to get the team to throw things away. An annual cleanup day may be just the ticket. Casual attire. Pizza. Plenty of trash barrels. Then award prizes for the "most improved." Don't miss the opportunity to reiterate the goals and objectives for the year. Use this time to talk with your staff about new procedures and ideas to make everyone more successful.

"Marriage is not just spiritual communion, it is also remembering to take out the trash."

—Dr. Joyce Brothers